HOW TO BECOME THE PERSON
YOU WERE MEANT TO BE

The Living as a Christian series:

Basic Christian Maturity

Growing in Faith
  Steve Clark
Knowing God's Will
  Steve Clark
Decision to Love
  Ken Wilson
God First
  Ken Wilson
Sons and Daughters of God
  Ken Wilson

The Emotions

The Angry Christian
  Bert Ghezzi
The Self-Image of a Christian
  Mark Kinzer

Christian Character

Strength under Control
  John Keating
*How to Become the Person
  You Were Meant to Be*
  Peter Williamson

**Bert Ghezzi and Peter Williamson
General Editors**

How to Become the Person You Were Meant to Be

Peter Williamson

SERVANT BOOKS
Ann Arbor, Michigan

Book Design by John B. Leidy
Cover Photo by Four By Five, Inc.

Published by Servant Books, Box 8617, Ann Arbor,
Michigan 48107

Scripture quotations are taken from the *Revised
Standard Version*, copyright 1946, 1953 © 1971, 1973 by
the Division of Christian Education of the National
Council of Churches in the U.S.A.; and from the *New
International Version*, copyright © 1978 by New York
Bible Society.

Printed in the United States of America
ISBN 0-89283-098-0

Contents

Living as a Christian

In human terms, it is not easy to decide to follow Jesus Christ and to live our lives as Christians. Jesus requires that we surrender our selves to him, relinquish our aspirations for our lives, and submit our will to God. Men and women have never been able to do this easily; if we could, we wouldn't need a savior.

Once we accept the invitation and decide to follow Jesus, a new set of obstacles and problems assert themselves. We find that we are often ignorant about what God wants of us as his sons and daughters. For example, what does it mean practically to obey the first commandment—to love God with our whole mind, heart, and strength? How can we know God's will? How do we love people we don't like? How does being a Christian affect what we do with our time and money? What does it mean "to turn the other cheek?" In these areas—and many others—it is not easy to understand exactly what God wants.

Even when we do know what God wants, it can be quite difficult to apply his teaching to our daily lives. Questions abound. How do we find time to pray regularly? How do we repair a relationship with someone we have wronged or who has wronged us?

How do we handle unruly emotional reactions? These are examples of perplexing questions about the application of Christian teaching to our daily lives.

Furthermore, we soon discover that Christians have enemies — the devil outside and the flesh within. Satan tempts us to sin; our inner urges welcome the temptation, and we find our will to resist steadily eroding.

Finally, we must overcome the world. We are trying to live in an environment that is hostile toward what Christians believe and how they live and friendly toward those who believe and do the opposite. The world in which we live works on our Christian resolve in many subtle ways. How much easier it is to think and act like those around us! How do we persevere?

There is a two-fold answer to these questions: To live successfully as Christians, we need both grace and wisdom. Both are freely available from the Lord to those who seek him.

As Christians we live by grace. The very life of God works in us as we try to understand God's teaching, apply it to our lives, and overcome the forces that would turn us aside from our chosen path. We always need grace, and grace is always there. The Lord is with us always, and the supply of his grace is inexhaustible.

Yet grace works with wisdom. Christians must *learn* a great deal about how to live according to God's will. We must study God's word in scripture, listen to Christian teaching, and reflect on our own experience and the experience of others. Many Christians today lack this kind of wisdom. This is the need which the *Living as a Christian* series is designed to meet.

The book you are reading is part of a series of books intended to help Christians apply the teaching of scripture to their lives. The authors of *Living as a Christian* books are pastoral leaders who have given this teaching in programs of Christian formation in various Christian communities. The teaching has stood the test of time. It has already helped many people grow as faithful servants of the Lord. We decided it was time to make this teaching available in book form.

All the *Living as a Christian* books seek to meet the following criteria:

- **Biblical.** The teaching is rooted in scripture. The authors and editors maintain that scripture is the word of God, and that it ought to determine what Christians believe and how they live.

- **Practical.** The purpose of the series is to offer down-to-earth advice about living as a Christian.

- **Relevant.** The teaching is aimed at the needs we encounter in our daily lives — at home, in school, on the job, in our day-to-day relationships.

- **Brief and Readable.** We have designed the series for busy people from a wide variety of backgrounds. Each of the authors presents profound Christian truths as simply and clearly as possible, and illustrates those truths by examples drawn from personal experience.

- **Integrated.** The books in the series comprise a unified curriculum on Christian living. They do not present differing views, but rather they take a consistent approach.

The format of the series makes it suitable for both individual and group use. The books in *Living as a Christian* can be used in such group settings as Sunday school classes, adult education programs, prayer groups, classes for teen-agers, women's groups, and as a supplement to Bible study.

The *Living as a Christian* series is divided into several sets of books, each devoted to a different aspect of Christian living. These sets include books on Christian maturity, emotions in the Christian life, the fruit of the Holy Spirit, Christian personal relationships, Christian service, and very likely, on other topics as well.

This book, *How to Become the Person You Were Meant to Be*, is part of a set that deals with Christian character. One of the goals of our Christian life is to become more like Jesus. We all know words, such as loving, meek, and joyful, that describe the qualities of Jesus. But we need help, not only in determining what these marks of character are but also in knowing how to grow in them. *How to Become the Person You Were Meant to Be* and other books in this set define the elements of Christian character and teach Christians how to be transformed in the Lord's image and likeness.

The editors dedicate the *Living as a Christian* series

to Christian men and women everywhere who have counted the cost and decided to follow Jesus Christ as his disciples.

Bert Ghezzi and Peter Williamson
General Editors

Introduction

Some of you who begin this book will be very eager to read it because it offers to tell you how to become the right kind of person. You are dissatisfied or perhaps just uncertain about your life and want to know if you are headed in the right direction. Still others of you may face decisions that will shape your future. Very often young people are interested in reading about becoming the right kind of person, since they are thinking a lot about their future.

I know some of you did not pick up this book because of the title, but in spite of it. You were not interested in someone telling you how to become a different kind of person because you are, on the whole, satisfied with yourself and with your life as you now experience it. You are not interested in another self-help book. You know what you are doing, you know where you are going, and you do not really need someone to tell you how to try to improve yourself.

But if you are a Christian, what I have to say is important to you, whether you are happy and confident about the kind of person you are right now or whether you are not. Why? Because we Christians know that our success as human beings is not measured by how satisfied we are with ourselves. Whether we are successes or failures is settled not by our own evaluation but by the evaluation of someone else, namely, God himself. A man or woman could meet every goal he sets for himself or herself and could possess every external indication of success, but still fall short of what he was *meant* to be.

This book is not about becoming the person you always *wanted* to be, but about becoming the person you were *meant* to be. That is because Christians believe that God created the world. When he did so, he made human beings, not simply to pass the time, but for a purpose. He did not leave us, his creatures, to go our own way, but instead gave us clear direction about his intentions for the human race.

We are accustomed to thinking about God's direction for what Christians believe and for what they ought to do or not do. For instance, when we think about doing God's will we naturally think of the Ten Commandments. Many of us also give considerable thought to obeying God's direction for what to do with our lives. Should I be a carpenter? Should I be a nurse? Should I marry and have a family? If so, whom should I marry? Should I be a missionary, a priest, or a minister?

But knowing what to do is only part of the picture. God did not need to make human beings in order to get something done. He could have made robots if he only wanted creatures that could take orders and complete tasks. No, God made us because of something he wanted us to be—sons and daughters in a relationship with him. Only when we really understand what God means for us to be can we understand why he wants us to do the things he calls us to do. To know God's purpose for the human race will also help us to know God.

This book will explain the purpose for the human race God has revealed in scripture so that you can understand the kind of people God wants you and me to become. Then it will examine how to make this change. Before applying this to our individual lives, it will focus on God's plan for all his people. This is not a "self-help" book. God's way is different. *He* will change us. What we need to learn is how to cooperate with the change he is bringing about in us right now.

ONE

Adam, the Son of God

O ne day some Pharisees challenged Jesus to
teach about divorce. They wanted to embroil
him in a conflict between two interpretations of
the law. One party of rabbis taught that a man
could divorce his wife for almost any reason. Another party was more strict, maintaining that a
man could divorce his wife only for a good reason, and there were very few good reasons.

Jesus' reply, recorded in the nineteenth chapter
of Matthew's gospel, is instructive not only because of his specific teaching on divorce, but because of the way Jesus went about replying to the
question. Jesus did not discuss the conflicting interpretations of the law. Rather he recalled creation and the purpose for which God created man
and woman and instituted marriage in the first
place. God's purpose in creating us male and female, he said, was that a man and a woman
would become one flesh in marriage and remain
undivided. That is why a man may not divorce
his wife.

I propose to follow Jesus' example in the way I
begin this book. To understand God's purpose for
any fundamental aspect of human life, we should

begin our study with creation. Why did God create us? If we know the answer to this question, we know much about how we are supposed to be. Creation may not be God's last word on the subject—a lot has happened since the beginning of the world—but the beginning is the place for us to learn about God's original purpose.

Another New Testament passage sheds some important light on God's original intention for the human race. This passage is the end to a genealogy. I suspect that most of you are probably like me when you encounter a long genealogy. You probably skip over the list of "so and so begat so and so who begat so and so" and continue with the narrative of scripture that follows. If so, you probably missed the last verse of Luke 3 which concludes the genealogy of Jesus through his earthly father, Joseph. It ends with

Enos, the son of Seth, the son of Adam, the son of God. (Lk 3:38)

We all know that Jesus is the son of God. How many of you realize that scripture says that Adam was also the son of God? When I first discovered this puzzling statement, my inclination was to dismiss it. Of course Adam is God's son. God created Adam. God is the father of all creation, because he created everything.

In fact, God's fatherhood of Adam means much more than this. To understand how important it is that Adam is called God's son, we need to understand what the relationship of fathers and sons was like at the time the scriptures were written.

Fathers and Sons

The relationship between Jewish fathers and their sons in the time in which the books of the Bible were written was very different than most father/son relationships today. In those days, little boys were cared for almost exclusively by their mothers until the age of five or six. At that age a boy left the company of his mother and sisters and began to live his life in his father's presence. This was the beginning of the relationship which, if all went well, would be the most important relationship the boy would ever have. From then on, boys would spend their time with their fathers and learn by being with them. They imitated their fathers. The goal was for the son to grow up to be just like his father. The father would impart to his son his way of life, his wisdom, even his occupation. In Jesus' day, the rabbis considered it the father's responsibility to establish his son in life by teaching him the scriptures, providing him with a wife, and giving him an occupation.

So we can imagine that Jesus, for instance, spent much of his time helping Joseph, who was a carpenter, and learning the carpenter's trade. In the gospels we read that Jesus was known as "the carpenter's son" (Lk 4:22).

The son would eventually succeed to his father's position. The eldest son shared in the father's authority over the household as the heir to whom the family inheritance would eventually pass. As the son grew in maturity, he would gradually enter into the relationships his father had with other members of the village or community. An adult son could legally represent his father, and act on his behalf. The father shared everything he had with his adult son as he established him in his place. It was in this sense that the father said to the eldest son in the story of the prodigal, "All that is mine is yours" (Lk 15:31).

Adam's Relationship with His Father

When we turn to the story of God's creation of man in Genesis, we see that when God created Adam, God related to Adam as a son in the same manner that a Jewish father related to his son.

Then God said, "Let us make man [Adam] in our image, after our likeness and let them have dominion over the fish of the sea, and over the birds of the air, and over the cattle, and over all the earth, and over every creeping thing that creeps upon the earth." So God created man [Adam] in his own image. (Gn 1:26)

The phrase "image and likeness" is a phrase that indicates the likeness characteristic of a son to his father. This likeness was understood not only biologically—a likeness in physical appearance—but a likeness in character and way of life, a desirable similarity that would come through intimate contact between son and father. When Adam himself had a son, named Seth, the scriptures describe him as being "in his [Adam's] own likeness, after his image" (Gn 5:3). In the same way, God had made Adam to be in his image and likeness.

Adam enjoyed a very close relationship with God; God walked with Adam in the Garden in the cool of the day. God established his son Adam by instructing him, by giving him a wife, Eve, and by entrusting the Garden to his care. God set Adam in authority over the earth in his own place. That's what God meant when he told Adam to subdue the earth and to have dominion over all the creatures that live on the earth. Though the Garden and all creation belonged to God, who made it, he entrusted it to his son to govern and care for it on his behalf. Adam was over the Garden as the heir, the one in the likeness to the father, the one succeeding to the father's position.

It is very important for us to realize that Adam represents the whole human race. In fact, the terms "Adam" and "man," or "human," are interchangeable in the Genesis account of creation. Hebrew, the language in which the book of Genesis was written, contains no capital letter which would allow us to clearly distinguish the human race from the individual man "Adam." In Hebrew, "Adam" means "man," or "human." It is also true that most of what is said about "Adam" in the text refers to women as well as men. Indeed, Genesis 1:27 says, "in his image and likeness he created man, male and female he created them."

Both sexes are created in God's image and likeness.

What this means is that God was not just bringing a single man, Adam, into this relationship with him. Rather, in Adam, God created the whole human race to be his son. God wanted every human being individually to be his son or daughter. He also desired that all human beings be united, and in their common life reflect his image and likeness. That is, they should look like God. Finally, God intended that mankind be in a very close relationship with him and exercise authority over the earth as he himself would do it.

We know what happened. God had forbidden Adam and Eve to eat from the tree of the knowledge of good and evil. The punishment for disobedience was death. Adam and Eve disobeyed God's command and had to suffer the consequences. Death and decay entered the world. Adam and Eve, and in them the whole human race, failed to become the kind of representatives of God that God intended them to be from the beginning. No longer could the same closeness of relationship exist between God and man. For the time being, God's purpose was thwarted. The image of God that had been impressed upon Adam and Eve and the whole human race was marred and disfigured by sin. Subsequent generations would inherit their first parents' bondage to sin and the penalty of death. The likeness of God in us human beings, while not completely eradicated, was changed in such a way that we could no longer accurately represent the father as his sons and daughters.

TWO

Jesus, the New Adam

A few years ago I spent a week at a retreat center in the Blue Ridge Mountains. While I was there I volunteered to do some chores. The retreat center had only been in operation for a brief period of time so there was quite a bit that Frank, the director of the center, needed help with.

Frank assigned me to cut some lumber to size to serve as bookshelves for the library. He provided the lumber, a saw horse, a power saw, a T-square, and a measuring tape. Since I have had very little experience in even basic carpentry, I asked for, and he gave me, very explicit instructions. The bookshelf would consist of five upright planks that would be placed against the wall, with a long board underneath them and a board over the top. Between the long vertical planks would be placed 24 shorter shelf-boards which would rest on brackets that could be set at various heights.

Frank stressed the importance that all of the shelf-boards be carefully measured. Their length was to be 32 1/4 inches. If there were off by a quarter of an inch in either direction, they would either be too long to fit between the vertical sections of the shelf, or, if they were too short, they would fail to rest on the brackets. After urging me to measure carefully and to use the T-square to make sure the shelves were squarely cut, Frank mentioned that I need not measure every single board. If I cut one to the right length, I could use that as my model shelf and cut all the other boards to the same length. That was a simpler and quicker way to go about it, so that's what I did.

In a certain sense, that's what God sought to do in making our first parents according to his image and likeness. If he was to accomplish his purpose for the human race he needed to have some model humans through whom he could produce a race of sons and daughters according to his specifications. When his model humans fell short of his intentions for them (through their own fault rather than through the fault of the Builder) he needed to get another model of the right dimensions. He needed someone in his image and likeness capable of producing human beings suitable to be his sons and daughters. This is exactly what God did in sending his son Jesus, whom scripture tells us was sent as a second Adam.

Like Adam, Jesus is the son of God. We are used to thinking of Jesus as God's son, but let's look at some passages from scripture that describe Jesus' sonship in the same terms as Adam's sonship.

In many and various ways God spoke of old to our fathers by the prophets; but in these last days he has spoken to us by his Son, whom he appointed the heir of all things. (Heb 1:1-2)

As God's son, Jesus was different from all the prophets, wise men, and leaders God had sent his people in the past. This passage goes on to describe him as God's heir, just as Adam was God's heir, and just as the Jewish son was the heir to his father's house, property, and position. Jesus is God's heir.

Consider another passage from Hebrews:

Now Moses was faithful in all God's house as a servant, to testify to the things that were to be spoken later, but Christ was faithful over God's house as a son. (Heb 3:5-6)

Moses had authority because it had been delegated to him as God's servant. By contrast, Jesus has authority by right, not by delegation. He has authority over God's people and the things that belong to God because he's their rightful owner— the son to whom all these things belong.

Jesus, like Adam, bears the image and likeness of God the Father: "He reflects the glory of God and bears the very stamp of his nature" (Heb 1:3). So much was this the case that when the disciples asked Jesus to show them the Father, he said to them, "He who has seen me has seen the Father."

The only aspect of a father's relationship with his son present in God's relationship with Adam but not obviously accomplished in Jesus' earthly life is the father's providing a wife for his son. But even in this respect God relates to Jesus as a son. The New Testament tells us that Jesus is a bridegroom and the church is his bride.

Of course Jesus's sonship is different from Adam's. Adam was made; Jesus existed before creation. Scripture says that it was *through* Jesus that Adam and all the created world were brought into existence. Long before he appeared on our earth, the Word of God dwelt with God as his son. When the Father sent him, he who was equal to the Father in power and glory and strength and holiness, but obedient to him, became a human being and was called Jesus.

Jesus' share in God's authority is different than Adam's was. Adam was given authority over the earth and was told to subdue it. Jesus has been given authority over all creation; everything has been put in subjection to him.

> Therefore God has highly exalted him and bestowed on him the name which is above every name, that at the name of Jesus every knee should bow, in heaven and on earth and under the earth, and every tongue confess that Jesus Christ is Lord. (Phil 2:9-11)

Jesus also bears God's image and likeness differently than Adam did. Jesus, Paul tells us, is *"the* image of the invisible God." John tells us, "in him all the fullness of God was pleased to dwell." As the divine son, Jesus is the perfect expression or image and likeness of God himself. Every other likeness, including that of our ancestor Adam, takes its form from his. Adam enjoyed the same kind of relationship with God that Jesus has —sonship—but Jesus' relationship as God's son is infinitely greater.

But the fact that is important for us is that Jesus is a human being who is God's son, just as Adam was, and that Jesus succeeded in fulfilling the will and purpose of the Father where Adam failed. Fortunately for us, the effects of Jesus' success are greater than those of Adam's failure. Paul compares the consequences of the first Adam's sin with the second Adam's righteousness:

> Then as one man's trespass led to condemnation for all men, so one man's act of righteousness leads to acquittal and life for all men. (Rom 5:18)

Jesus, the second Adam, undid the first Adam's sin. God sent Jesus as his son as he had once made Adam his son. Jesus was tempted in every way Adam was and we are, but he did not sin. Just as Adam's sin and guilt infected the rest of the human race, Jesus' righteousness and his right relationship with God has been communicated to us. C. S. Lewis calls it "the good infection." Humankind, or whichever part of it accepts God's gift, can be restored to full sonship through Jesus.

Before discussing how what Jesus achieved is communicated to us, it is worth asking what Jesus did that Adam failed to do? Paul tells us:

> For as by one man's disobedience many were
> made sinners, so by one man's obedience many
> will be made righteous. (Rom 5:19)

Our first parents failed by violating the one command that the Father had given them. Jesus succeeded by doing everything the Father told him and only that. It was by obedience to God that Jesus attained the goal set for him. Paul writes:

> Christ Jesus, who, though he was in the form
> of God, did not count equality with God a
> thing to be grasped at, but emptied himself,
> taking the form of a servant, being born in the
> likeness of men. And being found in human
> form he humbled himself and became obedient
> unto death, even death on a cross. Therefore
> God has highly exalted him. (Phil 2:5-9)

Recall Satan's temptation of Adam and Eve: "Eat of this fruit. If you eat of this fruit you will become like God himself, knowing good and evil" (Gn 3:5). Our first parents counted equality with God a thing to be grasped at, even to the point of disobeying him and losing much of the likeness to God they had been given. Jesus freely relinquished his position at the Father's right hand in obedience, taking the lowest place, the place of a servant, to the point of death on a cross. For that reason God raised him to the highest place of authority, at the right hand of the Father, and Jesus entered anew into the full privileges of divine sonship. Meanwhile his death on the cross made it possible for Adam and his children to be freed of sin and its penalty.

Because a new Adam passed the test the first Adam failed, God could begin the human race all over again on a different basis. And he did. God made Jesus the founder of a new humanity, the source of a new creation. Yes, everyone and everything can find a new beginning in Christ. This new human race will ultimately bear the fullness and likeness of the new Adam. A new creation has begun.

> From now on, therefore, we regard no one from a human point of view. . . . Therefore, if anyone is in Christ, he is a new creation. (2 Cor 5:16, 17)

> For we are his workmanship, created in Christ Jesus for good works, which God prepared beforehand, that we should walk in them. (Eph 2:10)

THREE

You and I

How is the account of Jesus' obedience to the Father more than an inspiring story? What concrete difference will all this make in our lives? What does all this have to do with you and me becoming the kind of people God meant us to be?

The answer to these questions is the Christian message. Jesus' death and resurrection set us free from the power of sin and death. His suffering atoned for our wrongdoing so that we could be forgiven. After Jesus ascended to the Father, he gave the Holy Spirit to those who believe in him. Jesus will return at some point in time to judge the living and the dead, and to establish his kingdom in its fullness. These are facts which most of us are already clear on. But another gospel truth must penetrate if we are to grasp what Christ did and how this affects us. This truth is expressed in a verse from Paul's first letter to the Corinthians:

For as in Adam all die, so in Christ shall all be made alive. (1 Cor 15:22)

We need to understand what it means for us to be in Christ.

The place to begin is to understand what it

meant for us to be *in Adam*. We saw in Chapter One that Adam represents the whole human race. In fact, if you take the Genesis story of creation as simple history, at one time he *was* the whole human race. Let's examine this a little further. As father of our race, Adam in a sense *contained* all men and women. This was the way of looking at things that caused the writer to the Hebrews to speak of Levi, one of Abraham's great grandsons, to have been "in Abraham" (Heb 7:9). From this standpoint the total genetic pool from which we derive our various physical characteristics was contained in our first parents!

But there is more to Adam's fatherhood than a biological relationship. This is a dimension that modern people find hard to understand. God sees us as a *unit*—as Adam's family. Remember that Adam represents humanity. Scripture teaches that we are born into our first parents' relationship with God.

Part of this is because we're like them. Adam passed on to his descendents more than a physical likeness to himself. Adam and Eve passed on to us their character, their way of life. Each succeeding generation of parents has done the same. Much of what makes us human beings is what we receive and learn from the human community in which we grow up. Scientists tell us that even the ability to communicate by speech is not innate, but must be learned from others.

Adam and Eve passed on to us much that was good, for they were created in God's image, and some of that likeness remained in spite of their wrongdoing. But they also passed on personalities marred by their sin of disobeying God's command. Insofar as we are *in Adam*, we are in bondage to sin and condemned to the punishment that came to our first parents because of sin. We are subject to death, just as they became subject to death. If we are *in Adam*, Satan can afflict us, just as he could afflict our first parents because they willingly joined him in disobedience to God. We can see the results of sin in ourselves and in the world around us. Someone once said that the doctrine of original sin is the one Christian doctrine for which there is indisputable empirical evidence.

When Christ came as the New Adam and fulfilled the Father's will, a new possibility for the human race opened up: the possibility of being *in Christ* instead of being *in Adam*. This is not a relationship of physical descent, but of spiritual descent. By becoming Christians we are spiritually united with Christ and come to share in his righteous humanity. Just as we inherit Adam's image and likeness and the consequences of his fall by birth, so too do we inherit Jesus' image and likeness and the consequences of his victory by a spiritual rebirth. Paul writes:

> In Christ Jesus you are all sons of God, through faith. For as many of you as were baptized into Christ have put on Christ. (Gal 3:26-27)

Through faith in Christ and through baptism, we have entered *into* Christ. *In Christ*, we are sons of God. Elsewhere in the New Testament we are told that through baptism, we have died and been raised with Christ, and even have been glorified with him at the Father's right hand (see Rom 6:3-11; Eph 2:4-7, 13; Col 2:10-13, 3:1-4). We have *put on* Christ. That is, we *wear* Christ's personality and character, his relationship with the Father, and his victory over sin, Satan, and death. It's a little like having put on a new set of clothes, except it goes much deeper.

Another metaphor may help. It's as though the whole human race were gathered in a giant Boeing 747 superjet which had been hijacked and was flying full speed to a place we didn't want to go. We land to refuel and are rescued. All who wish can enter another Boeing 747 which immediately takes off and turns back toward the plane's original destination. In Adam, all of us were captured by sin. We were subjected to someone whose intentions toward us were evil, and headed for death and punishment. When we became Christians, we changed course. By turning away from wrongdoing and believing in Christ, a spiritual change occurred that united us with Christ. We deplaned from our seats in Adam, and found our places in Christ. Almost before we knew it, we were forgiven, placed under Christ's protection and governance, given a share in his righteousness, his Spirit, and his relationship with the Father, and destined for eternal life. We are in Christ Jesus.

In the Body of Christ

We discover that we are not alone in the plane we have entered. We are part of a people, a human community once again. Just as our parents and the human community into which we were born showed us a way of life, so the new community of those who are in Christ which will help us to learn a new way of life. In Christ, God is creating a new humanity, the body of Christ.

> For just as the body is one and has many members, and all the members of the body, though many, are one body, so it is with Christ. For by one Spirit we were all baptized into one body. (1 Cor 12:12)

So all of us who are in Christ form a single body, and Christ is the head.

Being a part of the body of Christ means many things that affect our lives directly and concretely. We are not alone. We are meant to be interdependent with many other brothers and sisters who are also members of the body. We are meant to share our lives with others just as Christ has shared his life with us. All we have belongs to our brothers and sisters; all they have belongs to us. We are meant to be one.

Perhaps this is the easiest way to grasp what it means to be in Christ. We are part of the body of Christ on earth, a new people. Our primary community is no longer that of all human beings—the life we share with those of our country, city, or neighborhood. These men and women and communities are in Adam, and human society which has not been redeemed by Christ is flawed by the same bondage to sin that we ourselves were subject to.

Now, our primary commitment and identity is with those who are in Christ. With them we are a new people which, in its life together, should reflect the image and likeness of God. Like God, we love all men and want to help them and be united to them. Our mission is to reach out to those who are still in Adam and to invite and urge them to enter into the body of Christ. This is what the first letter of John says:

> The life was made manifest, and we saw it, and testify to it, and proclaim to you the eternal life which was made manifest to us—that which we have seen and heard we proclaim to you, so that you may have fellowship with us; and our fellowship is with the Father and with his Son Jesus Christ. (1 Jn 1:2-3)

Sons and Daughters of God

In a passage I quoted earlier in this chapter (Gal 3:26), Paul says that "in Christ Jesus, you are all sons of God." Let's draw out the implications of this fact. In our new position in Christ, we are now sons and daughters of God. We share in Christ's sonship, and in a real sense, we share in his nature and destiny as God's son. Paul explains:

> But when the time had fully come, God sent
> forth his Son, born of woman . . . so that we
> might receive adoption as sons. And because
> you are sons, God sent the Spirit of his Son
> into our hearts crying, "Abba! Father!" So
> through God you are no longer a slave but a
> son, and if a son, then an heir. (Gal 4:4-7)

Paul explains that our adoption as sons and daughters of God is far more significant than a change in legal status, a transfer from the family of Adam to the family of Christ. We are changed from the inside! God sends the Spirit of his Son into our hearts crying, "Abba, Father." We have a new relationship with the Father. Jesus said, "If you ask anything of the Father, he will give it to you in my name" (Jn 16:23). Because we are God's sons and daughters, we have complete access to him through Jesus Christ.

Yet our new identity as sons and daughters of God and our new relationship with the Father is not the only astounding thing about what Jesus did for us. Paul says, "if a son, then an heir." In John's gospel Jesus says:

> "All that the Father has is mine. Therefore I
> say that he will take what is mine and declare it
> to you." (Jn 16:15)

In other words, we have the privilege of sharing in the Father's authority and in the Father's ownership of all creation. This is our right as heirs, as sons and daughters of God.

The conclusion should astonish us. Since the Father has given Jesus power and authority over all creation, we will reign with him if we remain faithful to him. We were born in sin, in the disgraced family of Adam. But now, as members of the family of Jesus Christ, our destiny is to reign with him for all eternity. Reflect on the way Paul sums it up in Romans:

> If because of one man's trespass, death reigned through that one man, much more will those who receive the abundance of grace and the free gift of righteousness reign in life through the one man Jesus Christ. (Rom 5:17)

The End Result

The result of Jesus' action is to restore the human race to the purpose God had for it in the beginning. God wanted us to be his sons and daughters who bear his image and likeness. Adam failed; Jesus succeeded. Those who are in Christ, who are willing to be changed, will be able to fulfill the purpose God has for them. Jesus came into the world to create a new mankind in himself. This is true for us as individuals, and also corporately as the body of Christ. The Christian people are the new humanity. Our life together should show what God intended the human race to be. We are the fulfillment of God's purposes for human history, the human race united with God and with one another in love.

The change is not yet complete. So far we have

only the "first fruits of the Spirit," and we long for the completion of the process (Rom 8:23; 2 Cor 5:1-5). The full restoration to God's image is what the familiar Christmas carol seeks when it says, "Adam's likeness now efface, stamp thine image in its place. Second Adam from above, reinstate us in thy love." But we will be changed in every way to be like him. "Just as we have borne the image of the man of dust, we shall also bear the image of the man of heaven" (1 Cor 15:49). Even our bodies will be changed; all susceptibility to death, corruption, and decay will be eradicated.

The plan of God for men and women in Christ is so amazing that some Christians have wondered if the end result is not greater than it would have been if Adam had never fallen! Instead of being God's sons and daughters through the man of dust, we are God's sons and daughters through the man of heaven, through the divine Word of God himself. God has snatched victory out of seeming defeat, fulfilling his purpose in a more wonderful way than anyone could have imagined. Thinking along these lines, someone many centuries ago inserted these famous words in the Easter vigil of the Roman liturgy: "O happy fault of Adam that merited for us so great a redeemer."

Other Christians have speculated that what was seen in the Garden of Eden was only the first stage of God's plan for the human race. Had our first parents proved obedient, God would have eventually brought the human race to the same kind of relationship he made possible in Jesus.

God has not chosen to reveal to us what might

have been. But what he has revealed is clear and undeniable: God did something awesome through Jesus. By gathering us in Christ, God has made us capable of fulfilling his original purpose—that we be his sons and daughters. He made it possible for us to become the kind of people we were meant to be, men and women in God's image and likeness.

FOUR

Spiritual Maturity

What does it mean to be in the image and likeness of God? What kind of person does God want us to become? I will try to answer these questions in the next few chapters. God's plan for us is that we become mature sons and daughters— spiritual men and women who have the fruit of the Holy Spirit. When we understand what this means, we will know better how to become the persons we were meant to be.

Mature Sons and Daughters

Christians often have the wrong image of being sons and daughters of God. We think about new-born babies or small children. We see ourselves as little children playing on Jesus' lap. Some of us remember the child's prayer, "Oh Lord, as your little children we ask you for the things that we need," and we retain this image as adults.

Such a devotion based on being little children before the Lord may help us be aware of our dependence on God, but this isn't a scriptural ideal of our sonship. The scriptural ideal is that of adult sons and adult daughters, men and women who are fully able to represent the Lord, even as they rely on him.

We should have the posture of adult sons in the time of Jesus. The adult son was succeeding to the role and position of his father. He was a man of dignity, strength, and maturity. An adult daughter was skilled, capable, and responsible—a woman who served competently and with dignity. These qualities should characterize us as sons and daughters of God. The model for us should be Jesus' relationship to the Father, not that of a toddler in an adult's lap.

A Process

It should be obvious from what I've said that maturity as sons and daughters of God takes time. I know some Christians who display signs with the initials P.B.P.G.I.F.W.M.Y. This means "Please be patient—God isn't finished with me yet!" This is completely right. We are in the middle of a process through which we are being made over into the image and likeness of God.

I'd like to draw your attention to a passage from scripture which talks about this process. Paul writes: "My little children, with whom I am again in travail until Christ be formed in you!" (Gal 4:19). Here, Paul was addressing the Galatians as his little children because they were much like infants in their understanding. The rest of Galatians reveals why. The important point for us is that Paul sees the life of Christ as something that needs to be formed in Christians. It doesn't come all at once. It takes work and time. We are somewhere in the middle of the process. It is certain that at some point in the future we are going to be changed completely into the likeness of the Lord Jesus. This hasn't happened yet. On the other hand, we already have received new life in Christ. The second Adam has given us a new nature, and we have begun to live a new life.

Jesus speaks to us about the importance of acting as sons and daughters now:

> You have heard that it was said, "You should love your neighbor and hate your enemy." But I say to you, love your enemies and pray for those who persecute you, that you may be sons of your father who is in heaven. For he makes the sun rise on the evil and the good and he sends rain on the just and the unjust. For if you love those who love you what reward have you? Do not even the tax collectors do the same? . . . You, therefore, must be perfect as you heavenly Father is perfect. (Mt 5:43-48)

It is true that we are already sons and daughters of God just by being Christians and by having the Holy Spirit. Yet Jesus is speaking about an aspect of this truth which we also need to keep in mind: we need to *act* like sons and daughters. Jesus is telling us to love our enemies, not just our friends, so that we may be true sons and daughters of our Father, who loves his enemies as well as his friends. Jesus is calling us to step into our Father's place and to do things like our Father does them. That's how true sons and daughters of God behave.

What Does It Mean to Be Spiritual?

At the beginning of this chapter, I mentioned that God wants us to become spiritual men and women. Let's examine what this means.

Many misconceptions surround the term "spiritual." Recently I saw a flyer for a series of mini-courses for "spiritual voyagers" at The University of Michigan. The courses offered included astro-projection, Zen Buddhism, meditation, a discussion group on the works of Carlos Castenada, and a course on mysticism. Obviously the people who put that flyer together understood "spiritual" to mean something that is esoteric, nonrational, supernatural, or quasi-religious.

As I was growing up I encountered a meaning for the word "spiritual" among Christians that had a negative connotation for me. I began to think of "spiritual" people as those who were involved in a lot of religious activities, who spoke in a pious tone of voice, and refrained from many things that most other people enjoyed. They were strict, humorless, and serious. I never actually knew many people who were like that, but I did meet a few. I concluded that I didn't want to turn out anything like them. This kind of "spirituality" was a kind of standing joke in my family. My father would say with more than a touch of irony, "So and so is more spiritual than I am. He doesn't read detective stories."

While I was in college, I was baptized in the Spirit. I found myself greatly desiring to be a spiritual man. I discovered that the New Testament never uses the term "spiritual" in the broad inclusive way that the "spiritual voyagers" at The University of Michigan did. Scripture uses "spiritual" to describe things that pertain to the Holy Spirit. The worship of other gods and spirits besides the Spirit of the Lord is not described as spiritual.

Like many other people who have experienced a release in the work of the Holy Spirit in their lives, I began to think that being a spiritual man meant possessing powerful spiritual gifts, or experiencing the Lord working in one's life in a dramatic way. I did in fact begin to experience the Lord speaking to me. I saw people healed in answer to prayer. I heard prophecies given and saw them fulfilled. Isn't this what being spiritual is all about?

Two passages from scripture prompted me to think more deeply about what it means to be a spiritual man or spiritual woman. The first is from Matthew's Gospel:

Beware of false prophets, who come to you in sheep's clothing but inwardly are ravenous wolves. You will know them by their fruits. . . . Every sound tree bears good fruit, but the evil tree bears evil fruit. . . . On that day many will say to me, "Lord, Lord, did we not prophesy in your name, and cast out demons in your name, and do mighty works in your name?" Then I will declare to them, "I never knew you; depart from me, you evildoers. (Mt 7:15-17, 22-23)

The teaching here is clear. Jesus says that works of power in the name of the Lord—even works that are really done by the power of the Holy Spirit—do not in themselves indicate that a man or woman is in a right relationship with the Lord. The proof is another criterion: "You will know them by their fruits." What did Jesus mean?

A few verses from 1 Corinthians 3 finally opened my eyes:

But I, brethren, could not address you as spiritual men, but as men of the flesh, as babes in Christ. I fed you with milk, not with solid food; for you were not ready for it; and even yet you are not ready, for you are still of the flesh. For while there is jealousy and strife among you, are you not of the flesh, and behaving like ordinary men?" (1 Cor 3:1-3)

Paul does not consider these Corinthians to be spiritual, even though we know they had an abundance of spiritual gifts and experiences. To the contrary, Paul considers them men of the flesh. Why? Because there is jealousy and strife among them. In other words, their way of life and their relationships prove that they are not spiritual men and women.

The scriptures teach that a spiritual man or woman is someone who has the Holy Spirit dwelling in them and whose life is characterized by changed behavior. A spiritual man or woman is someone whose very personality and character has been shaped and formed by the Holy Spirit. To be spiritual is to be someone whose life manifests the fruit of the Holy Spirit.

FIVE

The Fruit of the Spirit

Jesus said, "You shall know them by their fruits." What does this mean? What is "fruit?"

A good way to learn what a scriptural term means is to examine the different ways it is used in various passages. A concordance lists several dozen passages in the New Testament which use the word "fruit." By examining a few of these passages, we can learn much about the meaning of "fruit."

So, every sound tree bears good fruit, but the bad tree bears evil fruit. A sound tree cannot bear evil fruit, nor can a bad tree bear good fruit. (Mt 7:17-18)

Blessed are you among women, and blessed is the fruit of your womb! (Lk 1:42)

He who reaps receives wages, and gathers fruit for eternal life, so that sower and reaper may rejoice together. (Jn 4:36)

Every branch of mine that bears no fruit, he takes away, and every branch that does bear fruit he prunes, that it may bear more fruit. (Jn 15:2)

For the moment all discipline seems painful rather than pleasant; later it yields the peaceful fruit of righteousness to those who have been trained by it. (Heb 12:11)

The word "fruit" has a different meaning in these different contexts. The fruit of a tree is different from the fruit of the womb. The fruit of one's labors is different from the fruit of God's action in one's life. However, "fruit" has a common meaning in all these cases. The fruit of something is that which the thing produces.

Therefore, we can see that the fruit of the Holy Spirit is that which the Holy Spirit produces in the lives of those in whom he lives. Let's look at what the scripture calls the fruit of the Spirit:

The fruit of the Spirit is love, joy, peace, patience, kindness, goodness, faithfulness, gentleness, and self-control. (Gal 5:22-23)

These are the qualities that should be visible when the Holy Spirit is living in a person's life. You can recognize the Spirit's presence by these fruit. In fact, the fruit of the Spirit are God's own character traits. They become part of our character when his Holy Spirit lives in us. It is still difficult to understand precisely what this means.

What Are the Fruit of the Spirit?

Many Christians think that the fruit of the Spirit are essentially feelings that the Holy Spirit inspires in us. This is exactly what I thought for many years. I thought that the fruit of the Spirit were the result of good feelings that came to people who had surrendered their lives to the Lord. I wanted to have the fruit of the Holy Spirit in my life, and I wondered why I didn't have more of those good feelings, so I waited. I began to wonder if what scripture said was really true. Sometimes when I prayed for the Holy Spirit to give me love—feelings of love—I got them. I did experience warmer feelings toward an individual I had previously had a hard time loving. But at other times, I experienced no such change.

A friend of mine pointed out something I wouldn't have thought to look for. He suggested that I could learn something about the fruit of the Spirit by studying the opposite qualities—the works of the flesh. These qualities are listed in Galatians immediately before the fruit of the Spirit:

> Now the works of the flesh are plain: fornication, impurity, licentiousness, idolatry, sorcery, enmity, strife, jealousy, anger, selfishness, dissension, party spirit, envy, drunkenness, carousing, and the like. I warn you, as I warned you before, that those who do such things shall not inherit the kingdom of God. (Gal 5:19-21)

The works of the flesh can almost all be recognized rather quickly as things that people *do*. They are all types of behavior in relationships that God condemns and declares unacceptable. My friend showed me that the fruit of the Spirit can also be recognized as behavior. They are things that people do in relationships with others: love, peace, patience, kindness, faithfulness, gentleness, self-control. These are not just feelings but ways of responding to people and circumstances that are pleasing to God. They are ways that God relates to us. Thus love means caring for and serving others. Peace means being peaceable, seeking right relationships with others. God may sometimes help produce this fruit in us through inspiring us with different feelings. But the fruit are primarily character traits that are obvious in our ways of behaving. God uses a variety of means to produce these traits within us.

Character Traits

The fruit of the Spirit describe behavior characteristic of Christians, but they are not simply righteous actions or good deeds. The fruit of the Spirit are character traits, that is, *habitual responses* of love, patience, and self-control in our daily lives. A change in our habitual response requires a change in what we are like. In other words, a person who bears the fruit of the Holy Spirit has been changed not only in what he does, but in who he is.

This describes the kind of people that you and I were meant to be; people who have the fruit of the Holy Spirit: love, joy, peace, patience, kindness, goodness, faithfulness, gentleness, self-control. We are meant to be people who reflect these qualities in the way we respond to all of life—to those who oppose us as well as to our friends, in times of sorrow as well as in times of joy. The Lord wants us to be people who respond this way because we have been changed by the presence of the Holy Spirit, not just because we are constantly exercising our will to behave rightly. We are meant to be people in whom the Holy Spirit has produced a new character, a character that habitually responds with love, patience, faithfulness, self-control. This is how God responds to us. Since God lives in us by the Holy Spirit, he wants us to take on his own image and likeness, his own character.

Communal Character

There is one other point about the fruit of the Holy Spirit, one which is rarely mentioned. The fruit of the Spirit are meant to characterize groups of Christians. In fact, it would be reasonable to conclude that they were not even primarily intended for individual Christians. Both the works of the flesh and the fruit occur in relationships. Can I be guilty of fighting, jealousy, party spirit, or carousing all by myself? Or, on the other hand, can I enjoy peace, patience, goodness, or gentleness except in relationships with other human beings? I don't think so. Even joy is probably referring to something communal, rather than an individual's behavior. The fact is that Paul commended the fruit of the Spirit and warned against the works of the flesh to a *body* of Christians, the church at Galatia. Some of the other passages in the New Testament that mention such qualities even more clearly refer to a body of Christians rather than simply each individual Christian.

It makes sense, when we consider their nature, that the fruit of the Spirit are most clearly manifest in a body of believers. The fruit of the Spirit is that which the Spirit produces, and the Holy Spirit is most present in the body of Christ. The church, the body of Christ, is God's temple on earth, the place where God by the Holy Spirit dwells among men. Just as sin disfigured God's image and likeness in mankind as a whole, so the restoration of God's image through the Holy Spirit occurs in the body of Christ.

The communal character of the fruit of the Spirit makes practical sense. Someone who lived among people who were completely absorbed in enmity, strife, jealousy, anger, and a party spirit would find it hard to grow in love, patience, and peace. It would be hard for someone to grow in goodness, which could be better translated "generosity," when his neighbors were selfish and bent on exploitation. On the other hand, if someone is surrounded by Christians who manifest love, joy, and patience, it will be much easier for that person to be loving, joyful, and patient.

The communal character of the fruit of the Spirit helps protect us against spiritual narcissism—an excess concern for our own individual spiritual growth. Instead we must pay attention to building up our brothers and sisters in the Lord. We should desire to see God's image and likeness expressed in relationships, in the life of our church, prayer group, or community. If we want to grow in Christian character, we will want our primary relationships to be with other Christians whose hearts are set on bearing the image of God.

Studying Christian Character Traits

We should study what the scripture says about the fruit of the Spirit. The Spirit produces the fruit, but a deeper understanding of these qualities will help us change and grow. The list of the fruit of the Spirit in Galatians 5 is by no means exhaustive. Three similar lists of the character traits the Lord desires for Christians can be found in Ephesians 4:2-3, 32; Ephesians 5:1-2; and Colossians 3:12-15. Additional passages to consider will be listed at the end of this chapter.

There is much to learn about the scriptural understanding of these qualities. Simply looking up the English words in a dictionary can deepen our understanding of what each of those qualities means. Using a concordance to find other places these words are used in scripture can deepen your understanding even more. Finally, behind the English words our New Testament uses to describe them are Greek words which the New Testament writers originally used. Behind the Greek lie Hebrew words for character traits described in the Old Testament which the New Testament writers had in mind. An analytical concordance or books on the subject can help those of us who don't know Greek or Hebrew study these words and their meanings.

As you study Christian character traits in scripture, you will notice that most of them are ascribed to God elsewhere in the Bible. This is only appropriate since he is restoring his own image and likeness in us. Studying the kind of people that God wants us to be will teach us about the character of God himself. Studying the character of God as seen in the scripture teaches us about the kind of people we were meant to be.

For further study:

> Gal 5:22-23
> Col 3:12-15
> Eph 4:2-3, 32, 5:1-2
> 1 Cor 13:4-7
> 1 Tm 6:11
> 1 Pt 3:8
> 2 Pt 1:5-7

The following books can help us understand the meaning of the fruit of the Spirit:

Flesh and Spirit by William Barclay
New Testament Words by William Barclay
Richardson's Theological Wordbook of the Bible
Some Bible dictionaries are also helpful.

SIX

Is the Goal Realistic?

I suspect that some of you may have been a little disappointed when I said we were meant to be men and women formed in the likeness of God. You were hoping for something more concrete and more attainable.

You may not realize it yet, but having the character of God, the traits called the fruit of the Spirit, is a very specific goal. Love, joy, peace, patience, and so on have very definite meanings, in spite of the vague way those words are so often used. These qualities are so concrete that, if you know what they mean, you can tell in short order whether they characterize your life and the life of the body of Christians you belong to. God didn't leave us vague or ignorant about the kind of people he wants us to be. The other books in this personal character series will examine the meaning of the fruit of the Spirit in more detail.

Is this goal of becoming formed in the character of God really attainable? Let me state immediately that we will not be completely changed to be like Jesus in this world. A fundamental change has already occurred in our spirits, but our bodies remain in the image and likeness of Adam. They are mortal, perishable, and still subject to physical death and decay. Our bodies will not be changed until Jesus returns to fully establish his kingdom. Paul writes:

> Lo! I tell you a mystery. We shall not all sleep, but we shall all be changed, in a moment, in the twinkling of an eye, at the last trumpet. For the trumpet will sound, and the dead will be raised imperishable, and we shall be changed. For this perishable nature must put on the imperishable, and this mortal nature must put on immortality. (1 Cor 15:51-53)

Until this happens—until our bodies are changed to be like Jesus' body after the resurrection of the dead—we will still have to struggle with that part of our human nature that resists God's will. Scripture calls it "the flesh," and it includes all those tendencies to evil that lie within us. It is not our physical bodies themselves that we must struggle against, but all the tendencies to disobey God we will experience as long as we inhabit earthly human bodies. Fortunately for us, the power of the Holy Spirit has freed us from the necessity of following the urges of the flesh. Though we must do battle with the part of us that resists God, the victory can be won. We can overcome the flesh. Paul tells us in Romans:

> What the law could never do, because our lower nature robbed it of all potency, God has done: by sending his own Son in a form like

that of our sinful nature, and as a sacrifice for sin, he has passed judgement against sin within that very nature, so that the commandment of the law may find fulfillment in us, whose conduct, no longer under the control of our lower nature, is directed by the Spirit. (Rom 8:3-4, NEB)

It follows, my friends, that our lower nature has no claim upon us; we are not obliged to live on that level. If you do so, you must die. But if by the Spirit you put to death all the base pursuits of the body, then you will live. (Rom 8:12-13, NEB)

Our bodies remain subject to death. A tendency within us to do evil has been dealt the decisive blow, but has not yet been eradicated. So much for our limitations.

An Attainable Goal

The good news is that you and I *can* really share Christ's character in this life. If we do our part by obeying him and yielding to his action in our lives, we will manifest the fruit of the Holy Spirit. Our behavior, our attitudes as well as our habits, will change so that they are like God's— loving, joyful, peaceable, patient, kind, good, faithful, gentle, and under our control.

I am not saying that you and I will be flawless, never making a mistake, never slipping up in some small way from time to time. But I am saying that we can attain basic maturity as sons and daughters of God. We can expect the broad outlines of our personality and character to mirror the image of God closely enough that those who observe us (and who know what to look for) can tell whose sons and daughters we are.

I am not speaking about something that belongs only to extraordinary personalities, people whose God-likeness is demonstrated in dramatic ways. Nor is it something attainable only by individuals called by God to some special role of Christian service. I'm speaking about a normal, but true likeness to God that God intends for all his children. It *is* possible for your character to become like God's. Not only is it possible; it is God's will.

The remainder of this book will tell you how you can change and become the person you were meant to be. This will be expressed in five principles of spiritual growth.

SEVEN

The Principle of New Life

Many religions and philosophies are the products of the human race's efforts to reach God and to improve itself. Throughout history, men and women have sensed that they are not what they ought to be. They have sought to remedy human defects by devising many admirable laws, codes of ethics, and customs to help people live in a better way. Buddha's eight-fold plan of enlightenment, the rich ethical teaching of Confucius, the noble ideals of many socialists—all these are men's attempts to improve themselves through better government, education, and self-discipline.

Many good people who have only a partial understanding of the gospel have approached Christianity in the same way. They see the Ten Commandments and the teaching of Christ as a set of laws and ideals that provide a good way of life, a way to help man rise above barbarism and savagery. They view the Bible as a traditional and ancient self-help book which offers inspiration and direction to those with sufficient desire and will to live out what they recognize as true and just. In short, such people see Christianity as a way in which human beings can improve themselves. This

approach to Christianity is perhaps preferable to
the many contemporary philosophies that advo-
cate abandoning restraint and looking out only for
oneself. However, the self-help and willpower approach leaves out the heart of Christianity and the
first principle of spiritual growth.

This first principle is that *spiritual growth comes
from God, not from us.* Education in the Christian
way of life and self-discipline are important, and
even necessary. But scripture reveals that it is the
power of God that makes Christians new. God
does not merely maximize the natural endowment
we received from our parents; he makes us a new
creation in Jesus Christ.

A passage from 1 Peter gives us the first principle of spiritual growth, the principle of new life.

> You have been born anew, not of perishable
> seed but of imperishable, through the living
> and abiding word of God. . . . That word is the
> good news which was preached to you. (1 Pt
> 1:23, 25)

Peter says that all of us who are Christians have
been born again from a seed. A seed was planted,
a spiritual seed not subject to death and decay.
This seed is the word of God, the gospel that was
preached to us and which we believed. It is a seed
which grows in us and comes to fruition in Christian character. In other words, the reason we can
grow into the image of God is that the right kind
of seed, God's word, has been planted in us.

If a man and a woman have a baby and care for

it—by providing food, clothing, and shelter—and
raise it—by teaching and training it as parents
should—the eventual result is quite predictable.
The infant will grow up to become an adult human
being. On the other hand, imagine a man and a
woman adopting a puppy and giving it the exact
same treatment. No matter how hard they try, no
matter how good "parents" they are to their "little one," the puppy will not grow up to be an
adult human being. It would only be a dog. The
reason is that the seed is different. Human beings
and dogs develop according to the nature of the
kind of life that began their existence.

As Christians, the nature that we have received
is God's own life, the Holy Spirit. This is the
power at work in us, the principle that will determine how we end up. The life of God will
enable us to grow into the image of God.

We can do much to help this seed grow. We
can feed it with God's word. We can place ourselves in a Christian environment. We can water
it with prayer. But ultimately the seed of new life
that God gives us, not our own efforts to produce
virtue, will enable us to grow into God's image.
Paul sums up this truth in his first letter to the
Christians at Corinth. He says, "I planted, Apollos
watered, but God gave the growth" (1 Cor 3:6).

I think the best demonstration of the principle
of new life is the changes in character that occur
in men and women who have just become Christians. While personalities remain quite diverse,
one can't help but notice a pattern of change,
sometimes occurring regardless of whether any-

one is teaching them the Christian way of life. Young people become more respectful toward their parents and other authorities. Married men grow conscious of their family responsibilities. Often new Christians try to clean up their speech, even before they quite know what's wrong with it. In many, an instinct to be generous with their money arises.

Not all the necessary changes occur spontaneously. Occasionally individuals show no change in the area they most need it. Nevertheless it is my experience that even in new Christians who have a long way to go, the new life of Jesus Christ can be discerned without too much difficulty.

Since it is God's life inside us that will enable us to turn out as we should, we should approach spiritual growth mainly by faith. We should have faith in what God has already done to make us his sons and daughters by implanting the seed of his new life. We don't need to rely on a self-improvement program of our own devising in order to obtain spiritual maturity. We can trust the Lord. Though it helps to study Christian character traits, our growth into the image of God does not depend on our intellectual efforts or abilities, but on God's determination to change us. And he is determined! Consider this verse from Romans:

> For from the very beginning God decided that those who came to him—and all along he knew who would—should become like his Son, so that his Son would be the First, with many brothers. (Rom 8:29, *Living Bible*)

When you put your confidence in the new life God has placed within you, you will see in your own life that spiritual growth comes from God, and that he is changing you into the likeness of his Son. You will also be ready to make use of the second principle of spiritual growth.

EIGHT

Putting Off and Putting On

The second principle of spiritual growth is *putting off the old man and putting on the new.* The basis of this principle is contained in the following verses from Ephesians and Colossians:

> Put off the old man which belongs to your former manner of life and is corrupt through deceitful lusts, and be renewed in the spirit of your minds, and put on the new nature, created after the likeness of God in true righteousness and holiness. (Eph 4:22-24)

This principle of spiritual growth involves *acting* on the basis of the change God has brought about in us. If we believe in what God has done in us, we can decide to behave differently. We can decide to exchange our old ways for new ways which are appropriate for sons and daughters of God.

Earlier we talked about "the flesh," that part of us that resists God. Here that part of us is referred to as "the old man," or "the old self," or "the old nature," depending on what translation you use. This is the sinful human nature we received from Adam. Now that we are in Christ, we have a new nature, a new self that is in the likeness of God and wants to do his will. Living the Christian life can be seen as daily deciding to put off the old man—that part of us that resists God's will, Adam—and to put on the new man, Jesus Christ.

I once had a professor of New Testament who summarized Paul's writing on Christian behavior as saying: "Become what you are!" Since we are now sons and daughters of God, born anew in Christ, all that remains is for us is to act accordingly.

This isn't so strange as it sounds at first. A carpenter friend of mine was hired to work with a crew of other men in repairing houses. Soon, however, the boss recognized my friend's ability and began to give him greater responsibility. Soon he was put in charge of the whole crew—including men who had worked there much longer than he had. My friend was the boss, but now he had to take charge. This was difficult because the other men were not used to taking orders from him. My friend had the title of boss, but he had to *act* as the boss before his new title made any difference. In other words, he had to *become* what he already was.

Specifically, putting off the old nature means stopping the wrongdoing that is a part of the old way of life. We must end those ways of behaving—not doing them, not talking about them, not thinking about them. We must leave our old way of life completely behind.

Just so there's no mistake about what kinds of

behavior and character traits belong to the old nature, the practical apostle Paul supplies several lists in his epistles. I am going to give you a list from Ephesians 4 and 5. The traits of the old nature, Paul said, include:

Lying
Sinning through anger
Stealing
Evil talk
Bitterness and wrath
Clamor and slander (loud quarreling and speaking against others)
Malice (evil intentions toward others)
Fornication and impurity (sexual immorality)
Covetousness (greed, desiring wealth or possessions that don't belong to you)
Filthiness, silly talk, levity (sexually suggestive speech)
Getting drunk

Elsewhere Paul supplies contrasting lists of character traits that belong to our new nature in Jesus Christ. Here's what Paul says in Colossians (interspersed with explanatory paraphrase):

Put on then, as God's chosen ones, holy and beloved, compassion, kindness, lowliness, meekness, and patience, forbearing [putting up with] one another and, if one has a complaint against another, forgiving each other. . . . Above all these put on love. . . . Let the peace of Christ rule in your hearts. . . . Be thankful. Let the

word of Christ dwell in you richly [constantly
listen to and speak to one another God's word].
. . . In word or deed, do everything in the
name of the Lord Jesus [do everything in his
person, on his behalf, in his Spirit, with his
authority, as his representative]. (Col 3:12-17)

These are the character traits which belong to
Christ's nature. Compassion, peace, patience, and
love fit his nature just as surely as anger, drunken-
ness, covetousness, and evil talk fit the nature of
the old man. Putting off the old man means putting on the new. Since we are in Christ we ought
to put on his character.

It helps to put faith in what the scripture says
to us about our spiritual condition in Christ. A
friend of mine had entered into a great time of
struggle in living the Christian life. It seemed to
him that all of his old ways were returning. He felt
oppressed by temptations from his former way of
life that he didn't feel he had the strength to
handle, especially anger. One day he was reading
a book by Watchman Nee entitled *The Normal
Christian Life*. He came across Nee's description of
the profound impact a passage from scripture had
on him when he grasped its meaning and put his
faith in it. The passage was from Romans 6.

Do you not know that all of us who have been
baptized into Christ Jesus were baptized into
his death. . . . We know that our old self was
crucified with him so that the sinful body might
be destroyed, and we might no longer be en-

slaved to sin. For he who has died is freed from sin. . . . So you also must consider yourselves dead to sin and alive to God in Christ Jesus. (Rom 6:3, 6-7, 11)

When my friend understood the passage he knew that the old self, the man in the image and likeness of Adam, the man who was in bondage to sin, had truly died in Jesus' death. He knew that no longer did he have to be subject to temptation in the way he once was. The old man was dead. The new man was alive in God and freed from the power of sin. He *could* be free of his old way of life, so he decided to be. It takes exercising faith in God's word to "become what you are" in Christ.

It helps to know that God's power is at work in us. Another friend of mine had been struggling with sexual temptation. He was afflicted with a seemingly irresistable temptation to get into a sexual relationship with a woman he wasn't married to. In desperation he prayed, and a verse from a psalm he read that morning came to mind: "The Lord is my strength." He remembered that God had given the Holy Spirit to dwell within him. What he needed to do to resist the temptation was to rely on the presence of God and the strength of God inside him. He knew he had God's power within him to enable him to behave as a son of God.

Often Christians focus on getting rid of the negative traits and the character of the old self. But I have found that it's equally helpful to think about putting on the character traits of our new nature. I know a man who had difficulty with fear and timidity. He made little progress when he simply tried to follow my exhortation to put aside his fear and to resist it. Sometimes that even seemed to intensify his fear. However, he started to overcome his problem when he sensed the Lord telling him to be confident, bold, and courageous. It was easier for him to embrace confidence and bold- ness as the traits that were appropriate to a son of God when he realized that was part of his new na- ture in Christ. In the same way Paul told Timothy, "God did not give us a spirit of timidity, but of power and love and self-control. Do not be ashamed then of testifying to our Lord" (2 Tim 1:7-8).

To me, the most striking thing about this prin- ciple of spiritual growth is how simply it is put in the New Testament. Put off the old man with its bad habits and put on the new man with its good habits. There is no complicated explanation of how to do it, and no apologies for how difficult it will be. The scripture just expects that because of the new life we've received, we have the power to put off the old life and to put on the new.

In this way scripture makes it a matter of our own choice. As Christians we have the freedom either to yield ourselves to the flesh, the old man, or to yield ourselves to the Spirit of Christ. For those of us who find ourselves struggling to do the right thing, it can be helpful to recall the perspective that scripture gives us. The power to do right is ours. Let us put on Jesus Christ.

NINE

Communion with God

The third principle of spiritual growth is *the principle of communion with God*. The basis of this principle is a passage from 2 Corinthians.

> And we all, with unveiled face, beholding the glory of the Lord, are being changed into his likeness from one degree of glory to another; for this comes from the Lord who is the Spirit. (2 Cor 3:18)

The apostle Paul is saying that when Christians come into God's presence we are gazing on God and are being changed by that experience. Of course Paul doesn't mean that we literally see God with our eyes. But if we know the truth of the gospel and are united to God through Jesus in the Holy Spirit, we know and experience him in a remarkable way. As we stand before God, he's changing us "from one degree of glory to another."

All of us have seen how one person can grow to resemble another by being in his or her presence. This is a natural human principle of change as well as a spiritual principle. For example, people who have lived together for many years often develop the same ways of thinking, talking, and acting. All parents have had the experience of seeing their children reflect their own habits and personalities—sometimes to their great embarrassment.

As I was growing up, I took on a lot of my father's characteristics without ever realizing it, both in regard to character as well as in minor habits. One thing I do just like my father is that I laugh very loudly. Once when I was in high school, my father came to watch me perform in the school play. The play was a comedy, and we presented it in a large auditorium which held about 2,000 people. On stage, surrounded by lights, I couldn't see past the first few rows of the audience. But I could pick out exactly where my dad was sitting, because he laughed loudly, and at slightly different times than anybody else. I do the same thing. On several occasions my friends have located me in a large crowd by listening for that same laugh.

Recently, I had a long talk with a friend I'm only beginning to get to know. The man, whose name is Mike, is of an unusually good disposition and character. He has much natural goodness. As I've come to know him better, I realized that many of his good qualities were in him before he made a commitment of his life to Christ. As we talked I asked him to tell me about what kind of man his father is. Mike proceeded to tell me. As he described his father's fairness, even temper, generosity, and wisdom, I saw very clearly how Mike got to be the kind of person he is. He had a very good relationship with his father and as he was growing up was able to spend a great deal of time with him. He absorbed his father's good qualities by spending time in his presence.

If human beings change by being in close relationships with one another, it shouldn't surprise us that we are also changed by living in God's presence.

Ways of Communicating with God

Because the Holy Spirit lives in us, it is a fact that our whole lives are lived in God's presence. Nevertheless, there are some particular ways of placing ourselves before the Lord that God can use to change us into his likeness. Here are six of them.

Prayer

When we pray we are consciously turning our attention to God. More than that, we are united to God by the Holy Spirit that he has given us. The fourth and fifth chapters of Revelation include the prayers of God's people in its description of the perpetual worship that takes place before the throne of God. Just as the ancient Jews used to go to the temple in Jerusalem to come into God's presence, so Christians, by means of the Holy Spirit, come into his presence through prayer.

The way many Christians do this is to set aside some time each day just to be with the Lord in prayer. Normally this time includes periods of giving him praise and thanks for his goodness, listening to his guidance, and making our needs known to him. The Lord's Prayer is a very good model for how to be before God in prayer.

However, turning to God in prayer is not something that we should limit to one particular time during the day. Christians should turn to God in prayer many times throughout the day. Paul says "pray constantly." The Jews of Jesus' day consecrated every aspect of their daily lives with various blessings that involved praising God. The early Christians continued this practice. A traditional Christian pattern involves offering prayers in the morning, at midday, in the evening, and at meals. Constant prayer of this kind is an important way of living our lives in God's presence.

Communing with God in prayer is one of the ways in which I most frequently experience God changing me. When I began writing this book, I was visiting St. John's, one of the United States' Virgin Islands. One day, as I stood on a lonely expanse of white sandy beach and looked up at a deep blue sky and the shimmering expanse of blue-green water that lay before me, I very naturally turned to God in praise. How could a man or woman do anything other than thank and adore God for the beauty of creation in its natural state? It was a moment when I had a deep sense of God's presence.

As I prayed, my thoughts turned to the troubles in the church and the world today. A desire welled up in me to be God's servant, to serve him in whatever way he wants. He desires the world to be saved, he wants the church to manifest his glory. I wanted to be his instrument. I promised him anew that he could have all of my life.

Hardly were the words out of my mouth when I became aware of an attitude of jealousy and competitiveness I had harbored toward a couple of my fellow leaders, and of judgmentalness toward a third. I had not been aware of that attitude until that moment, but in an instant I saw it clearly. I knew that the Lord had shown it to me so that I could get rid of it. I confessed it to him and resolved to be grateful for my place and my gift in Christ's body, no matter what gift or place he chose to give to others. I resolved not to judge someone whose situation I don't know, and when it is not my responsibility to judge. In a small but sure way, God changed me in those few minutes I spent in his presence on the beach.

Participating in the Body of Christ

Most people think first about individual prayer when they think about living in the presence of God. However, my experience is that many of my most profound experiences of God's presence have occurred when I was worshipping with a body of Christians. This should not be surprising because, as I mentioned earlier, the church as Christ's body is the fullest and most powerful manifestation of God's presence on the earth. Under the new covenant, the church is God's temple on earth, replacing the physical structure built by Solomon and his successors. It is when the Christian community is gathered that all of the gifts of the Holy Spirit are present.

But the body of Christ is more than an occasion

for worship with other Christians. It is where we are transformed by the presence of God as we unite our lives with one another. In the context of the shared life of Christians, many of the other means of being in God's presence become possible. God uses very human interactions with other Christians to change us.

Shortly after I gave my life to the Lord, I began leading a small group with a man named Bob. Bob and I clashed. I didn't like the way he led the Bible study, and he didn't like the way I led our common time of prayer. Our personal styles were very different and our theological views were strongly held and frequently opposed. Yet we had to work together. We were the only available candidates to lead the group of young Christians in the college dormitory where we both lived. God wanted us to love one another and work together. Later on it became clear that God was making use of the "sandpaper ministry" in the body of Christ to deal with some of the rough edges in each of our personalities. Today, many years later, we are fast friends because of the transforming presence of God in the body of Christ.

Christians who want to live in God's presence will find a way to join their lives to other Christians. In so doing, they will make the body of Christ a reality in their experience.

Hearing God's Word

When God speaks, his word contains more than just information or direction. Scripture teaches that God's word contains God's power. When God speaks, something happens. This is because God's word comes to human beings by the power of the Holy Spirit. When God's word is spoken, God is present. One of the best ways I know to place yourself in God's presence is to be eager to hear God's word.

We can hear God's word in many different ways. One way is through reading the Bible. Reading scripture is a way of placing ourselves before the Lord regularly and letting him speak to us, giving us whatever direction he desires. We "hear" him both through the objective general revelation of his plan and will contained in scripture, and in specific passages that the Holy Spirit draws to our attention.

God also speaks to us through the words of other members of the body of Christ. A talk or sermon will penetrate our hearts when it is given in the Holy Spirit and genuinely communicates God's word. Christian prophecy is another and very direct way in which God will speak to us. Often God's word will come through good Christian books or magazines.

When you hear God speaking, listen to what he says. Take it into your heart. Let it form the way you think. Let it order your priorities. Let it strengthen your faith. The goal is not simply to hear God's word but to *do* it. If God's word is to have its effect on us, we must obey it. If you receive God's word, you will find that he is changing you as you listen to him.

Receiving Communion

Different Christian traditions have different understandings about the Lord's Supper. However, most Christians agree on at least some important points. In 1 Corinthians 10 Paul writes:

> The cup of blessing which we bless, is it not a participation in the blood of Christ? The bread which we break, is it not a participation in the body of Christ? (1 Cor 10:16)

Paul calls the cup and the bread a *participation* in the blood and body of Christ. Other Bibles translate the word as *communion* or *sharing* in the body and blood of the Lord. Paul means that God uses the eucharist to unite us to himself. Christians call partaking of the Lord's Supper "communion" because it is an especially important way of communing with God. If we approach it rightly God will use this means to strengthen and renew the work of the Holy Spirit in us. It is a way in which we are deeply in God's presence.

Paul's advice to the Corinthians about communion includes a warning that is worth noting. Being in God's presence is a wonderful way in which God changes us, but it is also a dangerous position to be in if we are not in a right relationship with him. In the Corinthian church, many of the believers had gotten into the habit of receiving communion in an unworthy manner. They were treating the eucharist irreverently and relating badly to their fellow Christians. Paul tells them that

"that is why many of you are weak and ill, and some have died" (1 Cor 11:30). For them, being in God's presence became an occasion for judgment because they weren't in a right relationship with God. If communion is to draw us closer to God, we must be in an obedient posture before him. Christians cannot expect to benefit from God's presence if they come before him with serious wrongdoing of which they are unwilling to repent.

Using Your Spiritual Gifts

Each of us has received some gifts of the Holy Spirit for the good of our brothers and sisters in the body of Christ. When we employ these gifts in the service of others, God works through us. Many Christians find serving others with the gifts God has given them one of the best ways to be in God's presence.

I'm sure that many of you have had someone ask you about your Christian faith. As you answered, as you told them what Christ means to you, didn't you find that you received as much as you gave? God is present when we speak his word or when we provide some other even mundane service to his people.

The right way to use the gifts God has given us is in the body of Christ for the good of our brothers and sisters. In fact, we discover the gifts that God has given us only when we're with others and serving them. It is a distraction and an illusion to seek to discover one's gift apart from our relationships with other Christians. Serve where you are needed. Offer what abilities and resources you have. Let other Christians tell you about the gifts God has given you and accept their judgment about how you can best employ them to build up the body of Christ.

Suffering for Christ's Sake

Not too long ago I read a verse from scripture that I had never noticed before:

If you are reproached for the name of Christ, you are blessed, because the spirit of glory and of God rests upon you" (1 Pt 4:14).

Peter is talking about suffering that comes to Christians because of their faithfulness to the Lord. He says that the Holy Spirit rests upon us in a special way when we are spoken against because of our belonging to the Lord. Jesus told the disciples something similar when he told them not to worry about what to say when brought before authorities who would judge them for their Christian faith. "In that very hour," Jesus said, "the Holy Spirit will give you the words to speak." This is tremendously comforting. In the hour when we most need God's help, the Lord assures us that his Holy Spirit will be present with us in a special way.

We live in an age when more Christians have given their lives for the sake of their faith than in all the previous centuries of Christian history combined. Many who read this book will have the privilege of sharing in Christ's sufferings. If you do, know that you are in communion with Christ in the Holy Spirit and that this is a powerful way for him to be "transforming us into his likeness, from one degree of glory to the next." No wonder Jesus called Christians who are so treated "blessed" (Mt 5:11).

Should we seek to commune with God this way? We can do so simply by living out the Christian life faithfully. That will be plenty. Scripture says "all who desire to live a godly life in Christ Jesus will be persecuted" (2 Tm 3:12). It is virtually certain that if you are faithful to Christ's teaching, you too will be reproached for Christ's sake and get a chance to share in that spirit of glory that rests on those who are so treated.

Being in God's presence is not always a conscious experience. Nor are we always able to discern the changes he is working in our lives. It's a mistake to look too closely to see how you're being changed "from one degree of glory to the next." Sometimes our conscious experience is the opposite of progress in degrees of glory! Rather than depending on your experience, you should depend on what God's word says: "We all with unveiled face, beholding the glory of the Lord, are being changed into his likeness." The right way to approach it is with faith. As we turn to God with our lives, we can be confident that he is transforming us through the presence of his Holy Spirit in us.

TEN

God's Fatherly Training

The fourth principle of spiritual growth is that *God is actively at work in our lives to train us as his sons and daughters.* Like human parents training their children, God punishes us when we do wrong and allows us to experience difficulties that will mature us. Our Father in heaven is at work to change us into his image and likeness.

Anyone who has been a serious Christian for a while knows that this is true. But we don't need to rely only on our experience to recognize this spiritual principle; a passage from Hebrews explains God's training and directs us in how we should respond to it. Though it is a long passage, it is worth quoting fully here. This is my own version, a slight paraphrase of the RSV:

Do not forget the exhortation which addresses you as sons—"My son, don't be too casual about the Lord's training, nor be discouraged when he disciplines you. For the Lord trains those he loves and disciplines every son who belongs to him." It is for the sake of getting trained that you have to endure. God is treating you as sons; for what son is there whom his father does not discipline? If you are left without the training that all God's children receive, then you are illegitimate children and not true sons at all. Besides, we have all had human fathers who disciplined us as we grew up and we obeyed them. Shall we not much more submit ourselves to the Father of every living being and learn from him? For our human fathers disciplined us for a short time as it pleased them; but he disciplines us for our good, that we may share his holiness. For the moment all discipline seems painful rather than pleasant. Later it yields the peaceful fruit of righteousness to those who have been trained by it. (Heb 12:5-11)

You will notice that I use the words "training," "discipline," and "punishment" interchangeably. This is consistent with the scripture's use of these words. The discipline that this passage refers to is not just punishment for wrongdoing, but includes all training, much of which is corrective, that parents give to children and God gives to us.

How Does God Train Us?

The ways in which God goes about this training are almost infinitely varied. God has a way of finding just the right means to bring about the changes that you and I need to make in order for us to bear the image of his Son. The best way I can think of to communicate how God trains his sons and daughters is to give some examples.

A few years ago a couple who had been married for only a year or two came to me for counseling. The man, whom I'll call Bob, was at his wit's end about how to help his wife. Since their marriage, she had grown progressively hard to live with, more anxious than she had ever been before in her life, and very unhappy. Mary (not her real name) was afraid she had made a terrible mistake in committing herself in marriage to Bob. She was extremely vulnerable to emotional reactions of all kinds, even to the point of contemplating suicide. She had never acted like this before.

With the help of the Lord and some more mature Christians, Bob and Mary were able to understand what was going on. Mary did have some emotional difficulties, for which she needed Bob's support and God's healing. On the other hand, both Bob and Mary needed to make changes in the way they approached their marriage. Bob had a tendency to be passive and irresponsible regarding their common life as a family. Mary grew anxious when Bob failed to plan adequately and deal with problems in the family schedule. She had a tendency to take over where Bob left off and then become burdened with anxiety regarding the additional load she was carrying. Bob and Mary had complementary problems: Bob was passive and irresponsible and Mary had great anxiety to see that everything measured up to certain high standards she held up.

The result of our discussions has been that both Bob and Mary have made a significant change in the way they approach their marriage and their lives. Bob became more responsible and learned to follow through in his plans. Mary learned to trust the Lord and her husband, and in some areas to accept a more realistic standard for how some things should be done. In Bob and Mary's case, God used difficulties in their marriage relationship to help them become the kind of people he wanted them to be.

Another way in which God sometimes trains us is by increasing our responsibilities. A few years ago I reached a high-water mark in the responsibilities I was carrying at work and within the community I am part of. I was convinced I was handling as large a load as I could reasonably be expected to handle. I felt I was approaching the limit of my personal resources as I did the many things that had been assigned to me or that I had taken on voluntarily.

Just at that point, our community decided to send one of the leaders, a man who had substantial overall responsibilities, to serve in another country. Someone had to take his place, and I was asked to do so. In spite of my objections and recommendations of other candidates, my fellow leaders strongly urged me to accept this new responsibility. I agreed, but warily.

My added responsibilities helped me to make an important change. I realized right then that I didn't have the strength in myself to do everything I needed to do. I knew I couldn't solve the problem by trying harder. If anything, I needed to try less hard and allow God's grace to work more powerfully. So I said to the Lord, "Lord, this is up to you. You put me in this position. You know that I don't have the resources within me to handle this job as it should be handled. I can't try any harder. I'm going to try less hard, give what I have, and rely on you to make up the rest. In order to take on this greater responsibility, I need a greater measure of grace from you to fulfill it."

God did exactly that. I became more effective than I ever had been in my work—with less personal drain. God had used the circumstances to squeeze me into a relationship of greater reliance on him.

Often God's training is mediated through those who have human responsibility to train us. I know a young man who has learned much that is valuable for a Christian by working for a boss who invested time in teaching him to be a good salesman. My friend Joe has matured a great deal. He has learned a great deal about discipline, planning, and relating to others through this year of training on the job.

Parents have a very important role in God's plan of training. Christian parents who approach training wisely can do much to produce Christian character in their children. Unfortunately, too few parents realize the responsibility and opportunity God has given them. Or, if they do know about their responsibility, they don't know how to go about exercising it.

Another kind of training in the body of Christ is discipleship—the formation of younger Christians by men and women who are mature in Christian character and service. I regard this form of God's training as one of the most effective ways for us to become the people he wants us to be. Most of us have too little appreciation for this type of training. There is simply no better way to learn than having someone who is willing to teach you and correct and advise you when you need it.

Many of the ways in which God can train us seem on first appearance to be setbacks and trials rather than opportunities. As I was working on this book, I met a Roman Catholic missionary priest who told me about a serious heart attack he experienced five years before. At the time, he regarded this as one of the greatest misfortunes of his life, but he now considers it a great blessing because of the way God used it to change him. Before his heart attack, this man had lived a life characterized by running around, doing too much in order to please people. He often exploded in anger at his fellow Christian workers when his plans were thwarted. His heart attack put an end to all this. He developed a new style of personal relationships and a ministry that would enable him to live with his weakened heart. He also learned to depend more on God's power and to yield his will to that of the Lord.

Sometimes God's fatherly training is clearly punishment for our wrongdoing. I can share a minor humorous example of this from my own life. Often, however, it is a very serious aspect of God's fatherly training.

Some time ago I found myself receiving a lot of praise from other people, which, to be honest, went to my head. I noticed a certain rising sense of self-importance. I became too attentive to how I was appearing in the eyes of others. On at least one occasion, my service to some members of the community was less effective because of my vanity.

When I recognized what was going on, I quickly asked the Lord for forgiveness and forgot about it. That evening, however, I believe God administered a little discipline. The setting was a softball game between some of the leaders of our community. The previous year, I had managed the team to a come-from-behind victory. This year I was again given a responsible role: With the score tied, I was sent in at the top of the last inning to pitch. Usually I can do a pretty good job at slow-pitch softball. But in this game, the pitching rubber was set back two or three yards farther than usual. To my great embarrassment I walked the first two batters, gave up two hits, and made an error that allowed a run to score. After watching this performance, our team's manager graciously removed me. Everybody I pitched to eventually scored, and we lost the game by two runs.

The entire experience was humiliating. Almost all my fellow leaders, and a large crowd of community members, watched my performance. After the game, I made the connection with the vanity I had perceived in myself earlier. In a flash I realized that I had just received a good licking. I was grateful to the Lord for it. I had learned, in a memorable way, not to be overly concerned about how I appeared to others.

Not everything that goes wrong should be taken as God's preferred means of training or punishing us. In the case of the man born blind (Jn 9), Jesus taught that neither the man nor his parents had been the cause of this misfortune through their sins. Instead, God wanted to give sight to that man. He was blind, Jesus said, so that God would be glorified in his healing.

Normally when evil comes into our lives, we should resist it and ask God to remove it. If it's physical we should seek God's healing. If it's spiritual we should seek God's deliverance. If it's an obstacle to the Lord's work, we should consider how to overcome it. God wants us to fight in these circumstances, not to be passive. We often need the Lord's discernment about how to respond to setbacks that seem to be evil in our lives. We should seek this with the help of other Christians.

Occasionally we encounter instances of evil in the lives of Christians that we just can't understand, and which God, for reasons we don't know, doesn't choose to eliminate. Perhaps these sorrows are the consequences of sin which is still at work in the human race, or they are the direct work of Satan. Christians still need not despair. As it says in Romans 8:28, "For those who love God, all things work together for the good." God can and does use any circumstances—even those which are objectively very evil—to bring about good for those who love him and have faith in him.

I know a family of devout Christians who suffered a great deal as a result of an attack of rheumatic fever on a son when he was a toddler, which left the child severely handicapped. Their loyal love to that child and the grief it cost them have produced in the child's parents deep compassion and an outstanding Christian character. The epistle to the Hebrews tells us that the Lord Jesus was made perfect, which means complete, through suffering. In Jesus' case, the suffering was clearly inflicted by Satan and evil men, but allowed by God. In fact, enduring suffering was an important part of Jesus' fulfilling God's will for him in his earthly life. That can be true for us as well.

A passage from the letter of James teaches us how to regard burdensome circumstances of all kinds in light of God's fatherly training.

> Consider it pure joy, my brothers, whenever you face trials of many kinds, because you know the testing of your faith develops perseverance. Perseverance must finish its work so that you may be mature and complete, not lacking anything. (Jas 1:2-4, NIV)

From God's perspective, all the trials, difficulties, and setbacks we experience are designed to produce perseverance in our lives. This is a quality we need in order to be complete as Christians. God is gracious enough to see that we won't be without it. If we look at our trials correctly, they can even be an occasion of great rejoicing to us.

What's Our Part?

The passage from Hebrews 12 which I quoted at the beginning of this chapter says a great deal about how to respond to God's discipline so as to benefit from it. Being trained by the Lord, or by anyone else for that matter, is not an exercise in passivity. It requires that we actively respond. The following four attitudes taught in Hebrews 12 will help us to make the most of the training we receive.

1. *Remember that discipline is an expression of God's love for you as his son or daughter.* The main point of the teaching in Hebrews 12 about receiving training is that training (or discipline) is evidence that we are truly sons and daughters of God. Illegitimate children who have no fathers don't receive training. The fact that we are being trained is evidence that we are legitimate children of God.

When you're going through trials, know that God is acting out of love. His intentions for you are completely positive. When he allows difficulties to come to us, it is always for our good. Unlike human fathers, who may sometimes discipline impulsively or simply out of their irritation, God always "disciplines us for our good, so that we may share his holiness." God intervenes in our lives to give us training and correction out of his desire that we be holy as he is holy.

One final point about God's love: God is always in control. All the universe is subject to his power. He will not let us be tested beyond our strength (1 Cor 10:13). There are many things in this world that are not the way God would prefer them to be, things which he allows because of mankind's sinful condition, and which the devil perpetrates out of his malice toward God and toward the human race. Nevertheless, Satan is bound. Augustine described the devil as a bound dog. He has power, but only to the limits of his chain. There are limits to the evil that God will allow in our lives, and nothing that happens is out of his control. We can trust in God's love. He can and will take care of us.

2. *When God seeks to train you, pay attention and submit to his discipline.* The writer of the letter to Hebrews quotes from the book of Proverbs: "My son, do not regard lightly the discipline of the Lord." It is possible for us to ignore the training that is offered to us. When I was a sophomore at the University of Michigan, I ignored some very valuable training offered me by an instructor in an introductory history course—my major field. It was an honors section, allowing more personal contact with the teacher. The professor gave me a lot of advice about writing papers that I wasn't interested in. He sought from me a degree of seriousness about my study that I would not take the time for. Not only did I neglect good advice, but I did not get away with anything. I didn't go to the final exam because I realized I wasn't well enough prepared; I asked to take it later. My professor answered, "I'm awfully sorry, Mr. Williamson, but I will have to give you an "E" for the course. In retrospect I recognize that teacher as one of the better instructors I ever had.

Sometimes we relate to God the way I related to that professor. Many of us may someday regret that we failed to respond to God's training in our lives. We need to take training seriously in all the different forms in which it comes, including training and correction from those whom God has placed over us in our families, in our work, and in the body of Christ.

An important part of taking the Lord's training seriously is to submit. Hebrews 12:9 says, "We have all had earthly fathers to discipline us and we obeyed them. Shall we not much more submit ourselves to the Father of every living being and learn from him?" In short, the person being trained needs to be submissive. Training requires an authority relationship. We need to accept the Lord's authority over us when he disciplines us. This means letting go of our willfulness and seeking to cooperate with God. We must let him have his way with us. We must lay aside our various impulses, preferences, and opinions, and learn to follow his direction. A verse from Psalm 32 says it well:

> I will instruct you (says the Lord) and guide you along the best pathway for your life; I will advise you and watch your progress. Don't be like a senseless horse or mule that has to have a bit in its mouth to keep it in line! (Ps 32:8-9, *Living Bible*)

3. *Don't give up in discouragement but learn to persevere in training.* Recently, I was reading an article in *Sports Illustrated* about a professional boxer's chances of winning a big fight that was coming up in a few months. The author of the article was convinced that the boxer's chances depended

entirely on his perseverance during the grueling training regimen he was undertaking.

The lesson is the same for us. The writer of Hebrews quotes a verse from Proverbs which warns against two wrong ways of responding to the Lord's discipline: "My son, do not take lightly the discipline of the Lord, nor be discouraged, when you are punished by him." On the one hand, we can be tempted to treat the Lord's instruction too casually. On the other hand, we can be overcome by the rigor of what the Lord is requiring of us, and be tempted to give up. The author of Hebrews exhorts us not to grow weary or faint-hearted. How many of us fail to receive the benefit from God's training because of how hard it sometimes seems?

For me, the most helpful verse in this passage in Hebrews about God's fatherly training is verse 11: "For the moment all discipline seems painful rather than pleasant; later it yields the peaceful fruit of righteousness to those who have been trained by it." Scripture is quite clear that it will not always be pleasant when the Lord is dealing with us. In fact, it is often painful. The consolation is that later it produces righteousness in us. Later we come to share God's holiness. We need to wait for it. We need to endure, just as Jesus endured his own suffering:

Let us run with perseverance the race that is set before us, looking to Jesus, the pioneer and perfecter of our faith, who for the joy that was set before him endured the cross, despising the shame, and is seated at the right hand of the throne of God. (Heb 12:1-2)

Notice that the behavior required of us is not passive. We are to run with perseverance the race that is set before us. An active response is required: "Therefore lift your drooping hands and strengthen your weak knees" (Heb 12:12). It takes strength, courage, and the will to be victorious to benefit from God's fatherly training.

4. *Hold firmly to righteousness.* When we are being trained by the Lord, we will frequently experience pressure or temptation to wrongdoing. The writer of Hebrews tells us that the time when we are being disciplined is the time for us to be firm about right behavior:

Make straight paths for your feet, so that what is lame may not be put out of joint but rather be healed. Strive for peace with all men, and for the holiness without which no one will see the Lord. See to it that no one fail to obtain the grace of God; that no "root of bitterness" spring up and cause trouble, and by it the many become defiled; that no one be immoral or irreligious like Esau, who sold his birthright for a single meal. (Heb 12:13-16)

Specifically we are urged to maintain right relationships with others. This is what is meant by the phrase "peace with all men." It is easy for division to set in when the pressure is on, when there are difficulties in personal relationships that need to get worked out, when setbacks occur. These are the times when serious harm can come to a family, prayer group, or a church if bitterness is not dealt with and the grace of God is not sought for all.

We are also urged to guard against risking something of eternal importance, our relationship with God, our spiritual "birthright," by yielding to the wrong impulses of our bodies, in particular, sexual immorality. We are warned to keep God's commandments when the pressure is on, for this will prevent what is weak (lame) already from suffering greater harm, and will enable God to heal and strengthen us. If we strive for the holiness without which no one will see the Lord, if we make pleasing God our greatest desire, we will reap the benefits of God's fatherly training.

ELEVEN

Modeling Yourself on God

The fifth principle of spiritual growth is imitation: *We should imitate God and his Son Jesus, who is the perfect image of the Father.* This is exactly what Paul says in Ephesians:

> Therefore be imitators of God, as beloved children. And walk in love, as Christ loved us and gave himself up for us, a fragrant offering and sacrifice to God. (Eph 5:1)

Just as children who are in a good relationship with their parents imitate them, so God's children should imitate him. Paul says that we should observe God's character; we should learn how God handles things and imitate him. Then Paul says that we should imitate Christ and the way he lived. He loved us and he loved God. He expressed that love in the offering of his life.

If you pattern your life on God and his Son Jesus, you will become like them. People pattern their lives on others. All of us, consciously or unconsciously, have models whom we imitate. The scripture is saying here that we should make God our primary model.

There are some right and some wrong ways of imitating God. First, the wrong ways. The least dangerous mistake is to try to imitate God in his omnipotence, that is, in his all-powerful nature. Now if you imitate God in his omnipotence, you might try to remove yourself from where you are to a Carribean island where you could enjoy a beautiful vacation. You might decide to walk there across the Atlantic Ocean. The reason this mistake is the least dangerous is that you are likely to recognize your error before you get very far. You and I are obviously not omnipotent. God hasn't entrusted that to us.

A more serious mistake is to imitate Jesus in his place in God's plan. We all have different roles of service in the body of Christ. Some of us, especially those who have roles of leadership, are tempted to take on Jesus' role of savior for the people we care for. Without realizing what we are doing, we try to provide the complete solution to everybody's problems. Then we wonder why we are burned out, and why it all doesn't seem to be working.

The truth is that we can do only a certain part. We cannot be the savior and Messiah. That role has been filled by someone better qualified. True, the body of Christ fulfills Christ's role on earth. But we as individuals are Christ on earth only in respect to our role in the body of Christ. We can imitate Christ's service in whatever way our service corresponds with the one Jesus performed. We can preach as Jesus if our role is to preach; we can heal as Jesus if our role is to heal, according to the measure of the gift God has given us. All of us can love and serve our brothers and sisters. But each of us is only a part of the body of Christ and can imitate Jesus in our service only partially.

A third mistaken way of imitating God is to imitate Jesus in the special circumstances of his life. An example would be to decide to become a carpenter because Jesus was a carpenter. This example is not as eccentric as it may seem. It's not uncommon for Christians to decide to live a simple, rural life because Jesus lived this kind of life in Palestine. There may be good reasons to live in such a way, but it is doubtful that the Lord normally wants his people to imitate him in the particular circumstances of his earthly life.

Instead, scripture teaches us to imitate God's character—his habitual way of doing things. We described some of these traits in Chapter Five. Other books in this series will explore the basic character traits of God in greater depth. By simply reading the Old and New Testaments, and seeing what God reveals about himself and the way he does things, we can find out a great deal about the kind of people we should be. Obviously, we are not to imitate God's role of judging and punishing except where God has given us responsibility and authority, but on the whole we can learn much to imitate by reading the history of God's relationship with his people.

Throughout the centuries, one of the most intense desires of Christians has been to imitate the life of Jesus. Paul expressed his fervent desire to share Christ's sufferings and to become like him in his death and resurrection (Phil 3:10-11). This is a theme echoed by great Christians of all ages. After the Bible, the best-selling book of all time among Christians is a brief book of meditations by Thomas a Kempis entitled *The Imitation of Christ*. If you have never read this book, I recommend it to you.

The New Testament itself commends the example of Jesus to us in many places. I would like to draw your attention to some of the main passages in the New Testament which urge us to imitate the Lord.

First, scripture teaches us to imitate Christ's forgiveness:

> Be kind to one another, tender-hearted, forgiving one another, as God in Christ forgave you. (Eph 4:32)

It is the duty of Christians to forgive their brothers when they wrong them and repent (Lk 17:3-4), and to have a forgiving attitude toward all who wrong them. Remember Jesus' words on the cross, which Stephen, the first martyr, imitated when he too was put to death unjustly: "Forgive them, for they know not what they do." Jesus taught us the necessity of forgiveness in the Lord's Prayer: "Forgive us our trespasses as we forgive those who trespass against us."

Second, scripture teaches us to imitate Christ's love by committing ourselves to one another to the full extent of our resources.

> By this we know love, that he laid down his life for us; and we ought to lay down our lives for the brethren. But if anyone has the world's goods and sees his brother in need, yet closes his heart against him, how does God's love abide in him? (1 Jn 3:16)

Jesus loved us by dying for us. We ought to be willing to lay down our lives for our brothers and sisters, not only by dying for them, but by making available the resources we have to meet their needs. Jesus commanded us to follow his example in this regard when he said, "Love one another as I have loved you."

Third, scripture teaches us to imitate Jesus in the way he served his disciples. Jesus taught this kind of imitation in his own words. After washing the disciples' feet, an act of service usually reserved for the lowliest servant or the youngest child, he instructed them:

> Do you know what I have done to you? You call me Teacher and Lord; and you are right, for so I am. If I then, your Lord and Teacher, have washed your feet, you also ought to wash one another's feet. For I have given you an example, that you also should do as I have done to you. (Jn 13:12-15)

In this way Jesus offered himself as the model of Christian leadership. Jesus wants his disciples to see themselves as servants, leaders who will not seek their own advantage, but spend themselves in every way for the benefit of those for whom they are caring. Elsewhere Jesus says, "Whoever would be great among you must be your servant, and whoever would be first among you must be slave of all. For the Son of man also came not to be served, but to serve, and to give his life as a ransom for many" (Mk 10:43-45).

Fourth, scripture teaches us to imitate Christ's humility and obedience:

Do nothing out of selfish ambition or vain conceit, but in humility consider others better than yourselves. Each of you should look not only to your own interests, but also to the interests of others. Your attitude should be the same as that of Christ Jesus: Who, being in very nature God, did not consider equality with God something to be grasped, but made himself nothing, taking the very nature of a servant, being made in human likeness. And being found in appearance as a man, he humbled himself and became obedient to death—even death on a cross! Therefore God exalted him to the highest place. (Phil 2:3-9)

Like Jesus, we ought not to act simply to advance our own personal cause or for reasons of personal vanity ("empty glory" is the literal meaning of the Greek word translated here as "vain conceit"). Instead we should take on the attitude of a servant, looking out for the interests of others, not just our own. We should be like Jesus, who humbled himself (far more than we ever could since he was God at the outset) and was perfectly obedient to the Father and even to the human authorities placed over him. If we seek the highest place for ourselves, we will be humbled. If we have the attitude of servants, God will exalt us. Jesus is our model.

Finally, scripture teaches that we should imitate Christ in the way he endured suffering. We have already discussed the passage from Hebrews 12 which holds up Jesus as an example of perseverance. Another passage shows Jesus' meekness when persecuted for righteousness' sake:

> But if when you do right and suffer for it you take it patiently, you have God's approval. For to this you have been called, because Christ also suffered for you, leaving you an example, that you should follow in his steps. He committed no sin; no guile was found on his lips. When he was reviled, he did not revile in return; when he suffered, he did not threaten; but he trusted to him who judges justly." (1 Pt 2:20-23)

Jesus demonstrated a response to unjust suffering that runs contrary to all of our instincts. When we follow his example, we demonstrate for all to see that we are new men and women, transformed from the inside into the likeness of the new Adam. We are meek, not returning evil for evil, but desiring the conversion of those who wrong us and relying on God's judgment. Christ's example should also prepare us to suffer: "Since therefore

Christ suffered in the flesh, arm yourselves with the same thought" (1 Pt 4:1).

These, of course, are only a few of the ways in which we can imitate Jesus. A couple of years ago, I read through the Gospel of Luke specifically to study the character of Jesus and to find qualities about him that I might imitate. I recommend such a study to you. In the life of the Lord, we will find much that will help us to become the kind of people we were meant to be.

TWELVE

Conclusion

There is nothing more worthwhile, nor I believe more personally satisfying, than becoming the person you were meant to be. The remarkable thing is that this objective is attainable. In fact, God wills that you attain it. He wants all of us to be changed and to become sons and daughters who look like him, after his image and likeness. He has made this possible through the life, death, and resurrection of his Son. What's more, he has made it impossible for any of us who remain faithful to him to fail to achieve this end.

> For those whom he foreknew he also predestined to be conformed to the image of his Son, in order that he might be the first-born among many brethren. (Rom 8:29)

He has shown us how this change is to be effected. First, the death and resurrection of his Son has placed the principle of new life in us. Second, we must put off the old self corrupted by sin, and put on the new nature that is ours in Christ. Third, as we live in God's presence, his Spirit is changing us. Fourth, as a good father, he is teaching and training us through the circumstances of our lives. Finally, God calls us to model ourselves on him and on his Son. By God's grace, we can and will turn out to be what we were meant to be, men and women in the image of God.

By now it should be clear that God's plan is not just for us as individuals, but is intended for us as a people. He doesn't seek only individuals who look like him, but a people which looks like him. He wants his people, as one person, the body of Christ, to express his own character in their relationships with one another and with the world. Thus the task to be made over into the image and likeness of God is a task for churches and communities, not just for us as individuals. Because he is a holy God, we must be a holy people. Christ's personality and character must be incarnate in the church.

So the principles of spiritual growth outlined here are principles for bodies of Christians as well as for individuals. As bodies of Christians we can decide to live in God's presence, accept his training, and imitate his character. We can decide not to tolerate the behavior of the old man among us, and to put on the new man in our relationships with one another. We can discuss how we conduct our relationships together and what character traits we value.

Not only can we do these things in the Christian groups we belong to, we *must* do them. The degree to which any of us individually can become the persons we were meant to be is affected in this life by how much we as a body of Christians become the person we were meant to be. This is a matter for Christian leaders to discuss and consider. How can they shepherd their flock to manifest in both their individual and common lives the character of Christ, the fruit of the Holy Spirit? What is the role of Christian leadership if it is not to build up the body of Christ until we all together attain "to mature manhood, to the measure of the stature of the fullness of Christ" (Eph 4:13).

Paying attention to Christian character will not detract from fulfilling the church's mission in the world, but instead will enable us to accomplish it. Immediately after instructing his disciples in the Beatitudes about the kind of character he expected from them, Jesus proclaimed the dramatic consequences when human beings reflect the image and likeness of God.

> You are the salt of the earth. . . . You are the light of the world. A city set on a hill cannot be hid. (Mt 5:13-14)

The disciples who bear these traits, like salt, will preserve the earth from judgment and give it a flavor that is pleasing to God. Men and women of this kind will not go unnoticed by the world. Their difference is as striking as a light in the darkness. By means of their light, many who are lost will find their way. Let *your* light so shine before men that they may see your good works and give glory to your Father who is in heaven. May God help you become the person you were meant to be.

234.13
Wil

Williamson, Peter
How to Become the
Person you were
Meant to Be